C000242754

# 1812 Overture

—◉—

# Marche Slave

—◉—

# Francesca da Rimini

*in Full Score*

## Peter Ilyitch Tchaikovsky

DOVER PUBLICATIONS, INC.
New York

*Bibliographical Note*

This Dover edition, first published in 1996, is a new compilation of three works originally published in authoritative Russian editions. The Dover edition adds lists of contents and instrumentation and an English translation of the original prefatory text to *Francesca da Rimini*. The original note has been slightly expanded, and the Dante text is now given in the original Italian with a new English prose translation by Stanley Appelbaum. English translations have also been supplied for all Russian footnotes save two. These two footnotes—on p. 35, referring to m. 123, and on p. 57, referring to m. 202—concern "Supplements 1 and 2," not included here. They have been deleted from this edition.

*International Standard Book Number*

*ISBN-13: 978-0-486-29069-0*
*ISBN-10: 0-486-29069-7*

Manufactured in the United States by RR Donnelley
29069704    2015
www.doverpublications.com

# Contents

# Marche Slave
## [Slavonic March]

Op. 31 (October 1876)

# Instrumentation

2 Piccolos [Flauti piccoli, Picc.]
2 Flutes [Flauti, Fl.]
2 Oboes [Oboi, Ob.]
2 Clarinets in B♭ [Clarinetti, Cl. (B)]
2 Bassoons [Fagotti, Fg.]

4 Horns in F [Corni, Cr.]
2 Cornets in B♭ [Pistoni, Pst. (B)]
2 Trumpets in B♭ [Trombe, Trb. (B)]
3 Trombones [Tromboni, Trbn.]
Tuba [Tuba, Tb.]

Timpani [Timpani, Tp.]

Percussion:
   Snare Drum [Tamburo, Tro]
   Cymbals [Piatti, P.]
   Bass Drum [Cassa, C.]
   Tam-Tam [Tam-tam, T-t.]

Strings [Archi]:
   Violins I, II [Violini]
   Violas [Viole, Vle.]
   Cellos [Violoncelli, Vc.]
   Basses [Contrabassi, Cb.]

Moderato in modo di marcia funebre

3

1) **T. 64 В автографе: Cr. III. IV**

m. 64. In the MS:

1) **Т. 67.** В партитуре изд. Юргенсона: Pst. ; исправлено по автографу

m. 67. In Jurgenson's score: ; corrected on the basis of the MS.

L'istesso tempo

90

120

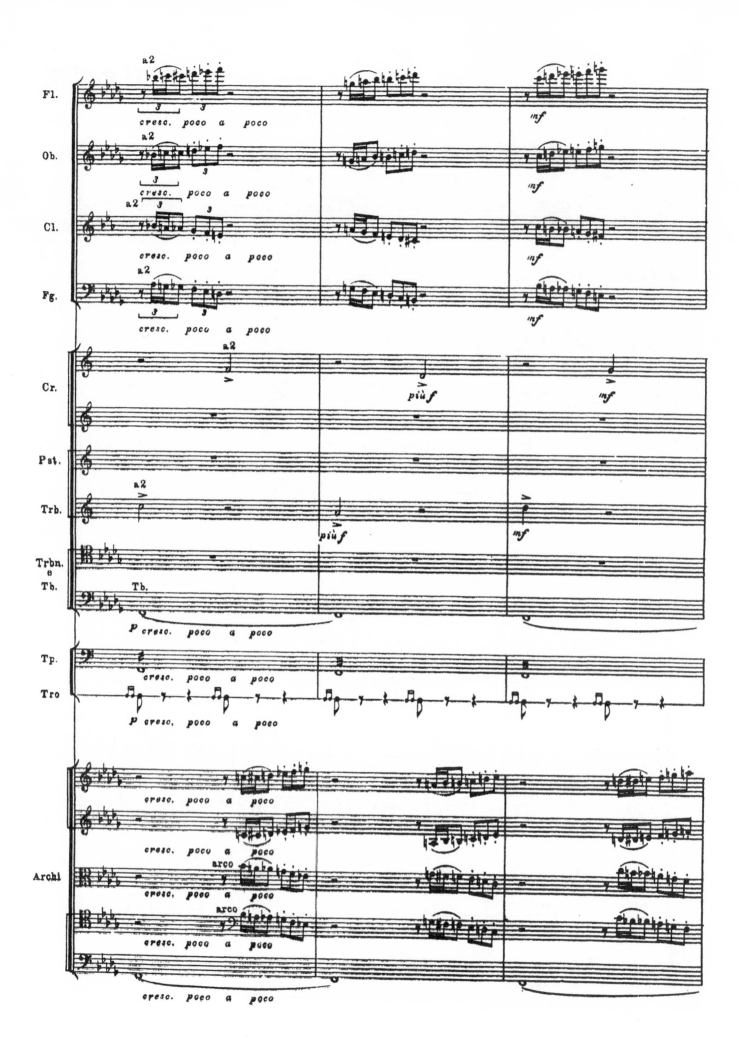

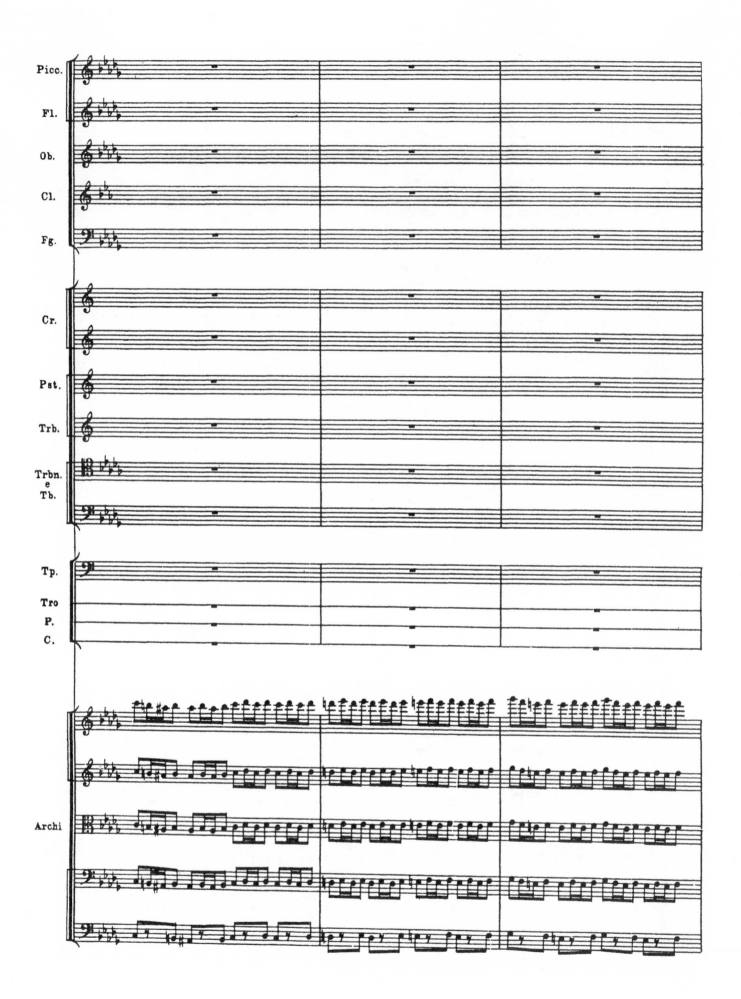

[to p. 61]

Marche Slave 65

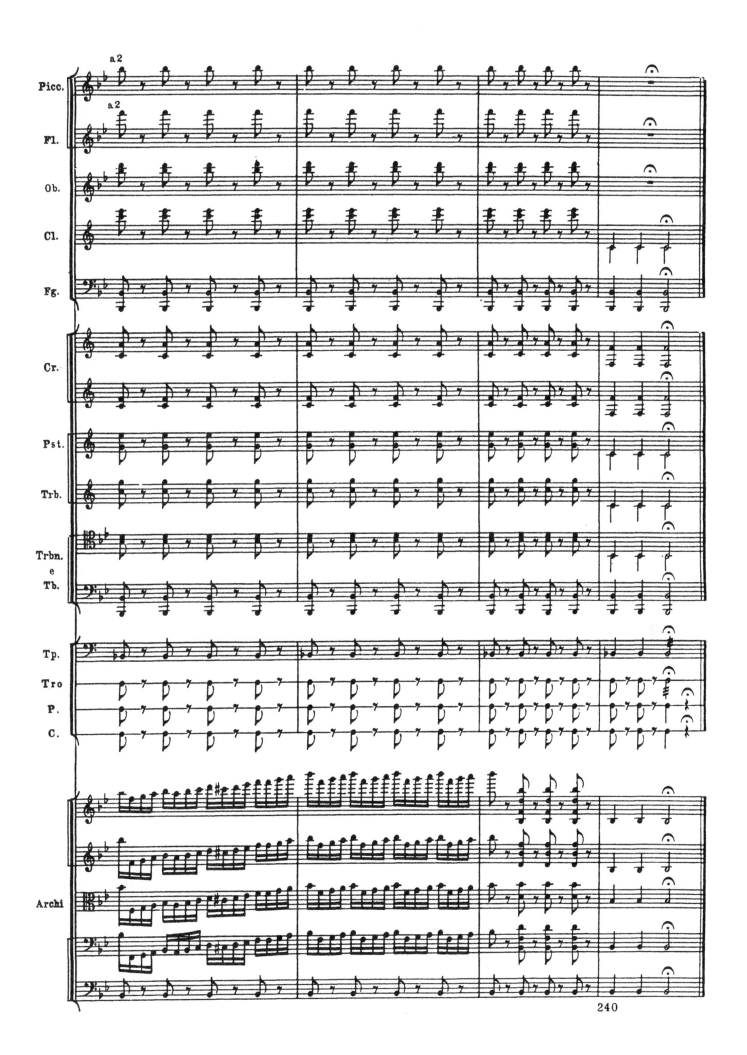

240

# Francesca da Rimini
## *Symphonic Fantasia after Dante*
### Op. 32 (November 1876)

In 13th-century Rimini, Francesca, daughter of Guido da Polenta, is murdered by her husband when he discovers her in adultery with his brother Paolo Malatesta, whom he also kills. The lovers are forever relegated to the second circle of Hell. Descending to this place, Dante there sees the punishment of the voluptuaries, who are tormented by an extremely fierce, uninterrupted whirlwind blowing through a dark, gloomy space. Among the sufferers he recognizes Francesca da Rimini, who tells him her story:

. . . 'Nessun maggior dolore
Che ricordarsi del tempo felice
Ne la miseria: e ció sa 'l tuo dottore.
Ma s' a conoscer la prima radice
Del nostro amor tu hai cotanto affetto,
Farò come colui che piange e dice.
Noi leggiavamo un giorno per diletto,
Di Lancialotto, come amor lo strinse;
Soli eravamo e sanza alcun sospetto.
Per piú fiate li occhi ci sospinse
Quella lettura, e scolorocci il viso;
Ma solo un punto fu quel che ci vinse.
Quando leggemmo il disiato riso
Esser baciato da cotanto amante,
Questi, che mai da me non fia diviso,
La bocca mi baciò tutto tremante.
Galeotto fu 'l libro e chi lo scrisse:
Quel giorno piú non vi leggemmo avante.'
Mentre che l' uno spirto questo disse,
L'altro piangea, sí che di pietade
Io venni men cosí com' io morisse;
E caddi come corpo morto cade.

. . . "There is no greater sorrow
than recalling happy times
in present misery: and your guide[1] knows this.
But if to know the original root
of our love you have such great desire,
I shall be as one who weeps and speaks.
We[2] were reading one day for amusement
about Lancelot, how love seized upon him;
we were alone and without any suspicion.
Several times our eyes were drawn together
by what we read, and our faces turned pale;
but there was only one passage that got the better of us.
When we read of how the longed-for, laughing lips[3]
were kissed by such a great lover,
this man, who will never again be separated from me,
kissed me on the mouth, all a-tremble.
Gallehault[4] was the name of the book and of its author:
That day we read no further in it."
While one of the spirits said this,
the other was weeping, so that from pity
I fainted away as if I were dying;
and I fell as a dead body falls.

From Dante's *Inferno*, Canto V

[1]Vergil, who is guiding Dante through the underworld.
[2]Francesca and Paolo.
[3]Of Queen Guenevere.
[4]The intermediary who brought Lancelot and Guenevere together.

# Instrumentation

3 Flutes [Flauti, Fl.]
  *Fl. III doubles Piccolo [Picc.]*
2 Oboes [Oboi, Ob.]
English Horn [Corno inglese, C.i.]
2 Clarinets in A [Clarinetti, Cl.]
2 Bassoons [Fagotti, Fg.]

4 Horns in F [Corni, Cr.]
2 Cornets in A [Pistoni, Pst.]
2 Trumpets in E [Trombe, Trb.]
3 Trombones [Tromboni, Trbn.]
Tuba [Tuba, Tb.]

Percussion:
  Cymbals [Piatti, P.]
  Bass Drum [Cassa, C.]
  Tam-Tam [Tam-tam, T-t.]

Harp [Arpa, A.]

Strings [Archi]:
  Violins I, II [Violini, V.]
  Violas [Viole, Vle.]
  Cellos [Violoncelli, Vc.]
  Basses [Contrabassi, Cb.]

71

Più mosso. Moderato

1) T. 40. В автографе и партитуре изд. Юргенсона у Fl., Picc. и Ob. лиги поставлены так:

m. 40. In the MS and Jurgenson's score, the slurs in Fl., Picc. and Ob. read:

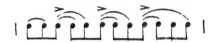

1) Т. 51. В автографе и партитуре изд. Юргенсона у Fl., Picc. и Ob. лиги поставлены так:

1) m. 51. In the MS and Jurgenson's score, the slurs in Fl., Picc. and Ob. read:

2) Тт. 52-53. В автографе и партитуре изд. Юргенсона у V.I и V. II лиги поставлены так:

2) mm. 52–53. In the MS and Jurgenson's score, the slurs in V. I and V. II read:

1) Тт. 64 - 65. В партитуре изд. Юргенсона:  Исправлено по автографу.
mm. 64–65. In Jurgenson's score:  Corrected on the basis of the MS.

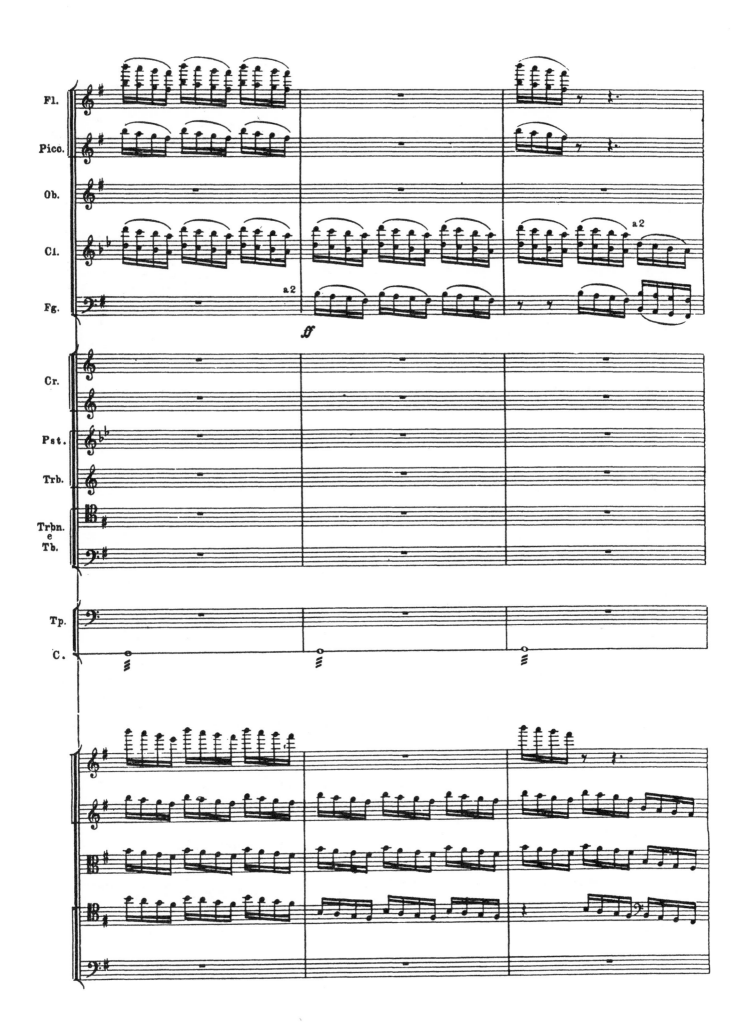

120   *Francesca da Rimini*

260

1) Т. 394. В автографе над строкой Fl. I указание: „*Leggierissimo*“.
m. 394. In the MS, over the Fl. I line there is the indication: „*Leggierissimo*“.

1) Тт. 547 и 551. В автографе и партитуре изд. Юргенсона партии всех четырех валторн отсутствуют. Добавлено по аналогии с тт. 94 и 98.

mm. 547 and 551. In the MS and Jurgenson's score, the parts for all four horns are missing. Supplied here by analogy with mm.  94 and 98.

1) T. 555. В автографе и партитуре изд. Юргенсона: Fl. II  ; изменено в соответствии
   с т. 102.

m. 555. In the MS and Jurgenson's score: altered to correspond with m. 102.

1) Тт. 567, 571 и 575. В автографе и партитуре изд. Юргенсона партия Piatti отсутствует. Добавлено по аналогии с тт. 114, 118 и 122.

mm. 567, 571 and 575. In the MS and Jurgenson's score, the Piatti part is missing. Supplied here by analogy with mm. 114, 118 and 122.

600

610

670

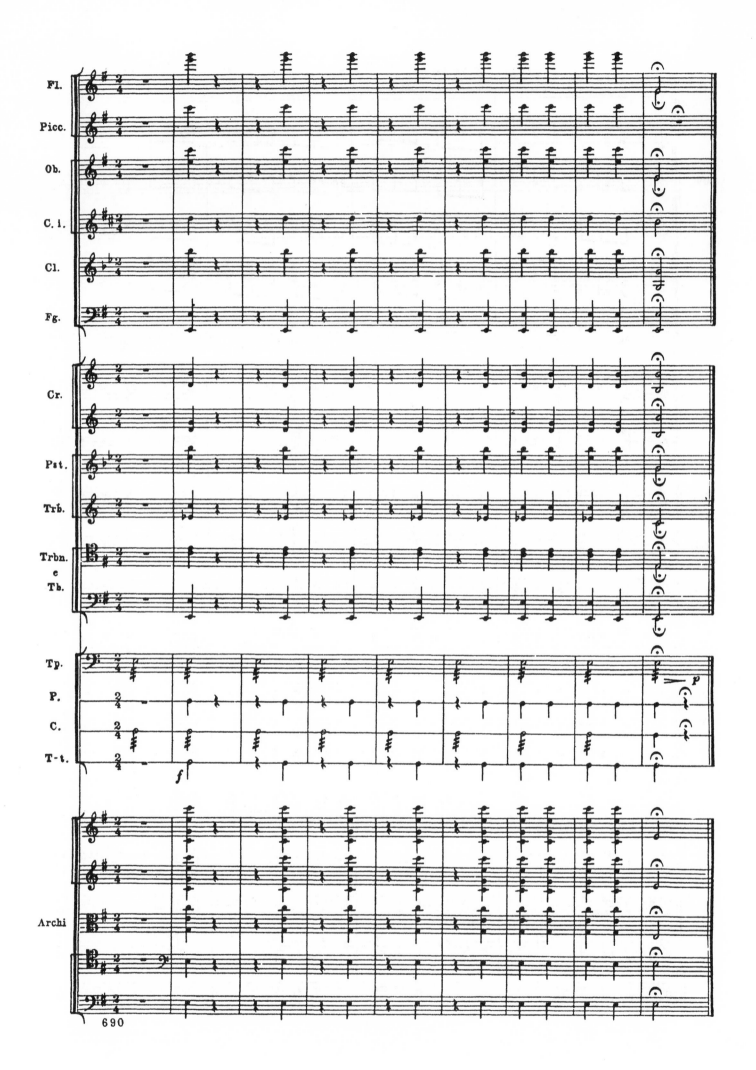

690

# 1812
# Festival Overture

Op. 49 (November 1880)

# Instrumentation

[Wind/Brass] Band, *ad libitum* [Banda, Bnd.]

Piccolo [Fl. Piccolo, Picc.]
2 Flutes [Flauti, Fl.]
2 Oboes [Oboi, Ob.]
English Horn [Corno inglese, C.i.]
2 Clarinets in B♭ [Clarinetti, Cl. (B)]
2 Bassoons [Fagotti, Fg.]

4 Horns in F [Corni, Cr.]
2 Cornets in B♭ [Pistoni, Pst. (B)]
2 Trumpets in E♭ [Trombe, Trb. (Es)]
3 Trombones [Tromboni, Trbn.]
Tuba [Tuba, Tb.]

Timpani [Timpani, Tp.]

Percussion:
    Triangle [Triangolo, Trgl.]
    Tambourine [Tamburino, Tno]
    Snare Drum [Tamburo, Tro]
    Cymbals [Piatti, P.]
    Bass Drum [Gran cassa, G.c.]
    Bells [Campane, Cmp.]*
    Cannon [Cannone, Cn.]*

Strings [Archi]
    Violins I, II [Violini]
    Violas [Viole, Vle]
    Cellos [Violoncelli, Vc., V-c.]
    Basses [Contrabassi, C-b.]

*Translation of original footnotes 1 and 2, p. 213:
  1) The manuscript and Jurgenson's score contain the notice: "The bells should be big; their pitch is of no concern; they should be rung in imitation of a festive pealing."
  2) In the manuscript, [the Cannon is labeled] "Bombardone"; the manuscript and Jurgenson's score contain the notice: "Instrument used in theaters to simulate a cannon shot."

1) В автографе и изд. Юргенсона есть примечание:„Колокола должны быть большие;строй их безразличен; бить в них следует, подражая праздничному перезвону.“

2) В автографе „Bombardone“ и примечание, имеющиеся и в изд. Юргенсона:„Инструмент, употребляемый в театрах для изображения пушечного выстрела.“

3) В автографе и изд.Юргенсона есть примечание:„Если состав оркестра позволит, то желательно, чтобы это место исполнялось 8-ю виолончелями и 4-мя альтами, по 2 на каждый голос.“

1) and 2) See footnotes, p. 212.

3) The MS and Jurgenson's score contain the notice: "If the size of the orchestra permits, it is desirable for this passage to be played by 8 cellos and 4 violas, two to each part."

213

1) Т. 79 над партией Ob. в автографе „Staccato"

m. 79. In the MS, over the Ob. part: „Staccato"

1) **T. 93 V-I** в автографе „*f*“
m. 93: V. I in the MS „*f*“

9 L'istesso tempo [1]

1) Это обозначение в изд. Юргенсона отсутствует.

This marking does not appear in Jurgenson's score.

220

1) **T.** 216  **Cl. I** в автографе „*p*"
   m. 216. Cl. I in the MS „*p*"

240

1) т. 278 Ob. I. II в автографе:
m. 278. Ob. I. II. in the MS:

1) т. т. **286 и 289 C. i.** в автографе:
mm. 286 and 289, C.i. in the MS:

2) т. т. **291 Cr. III. IV** в автографе:
m. 291, Cr. III. IV. in the MS:

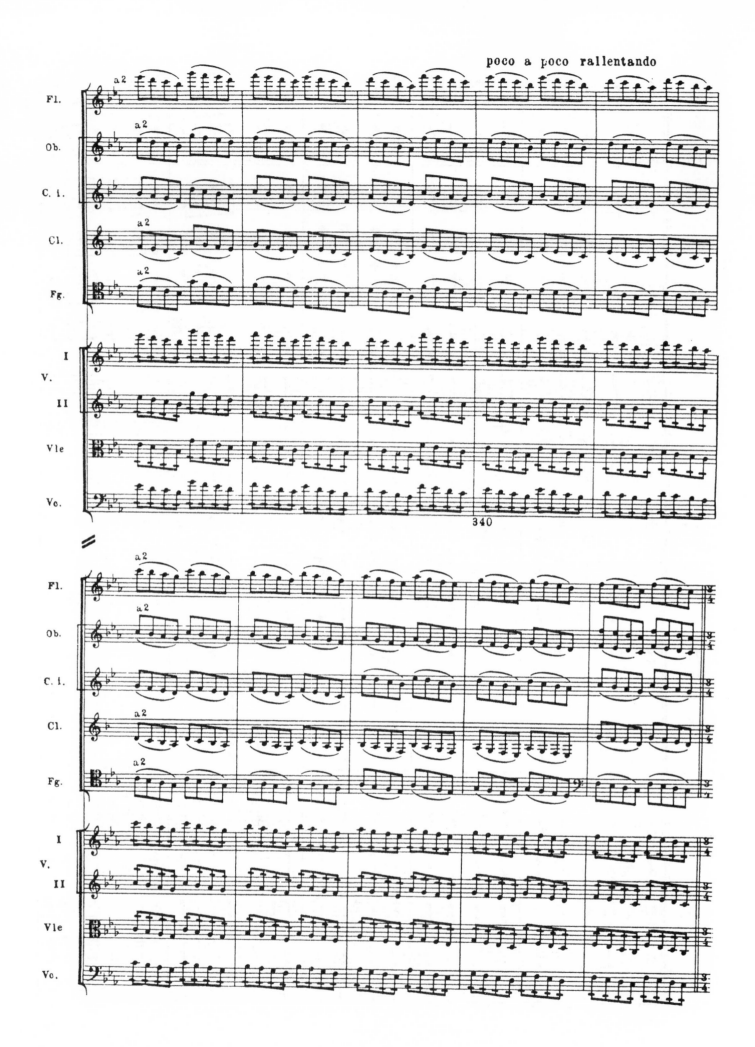

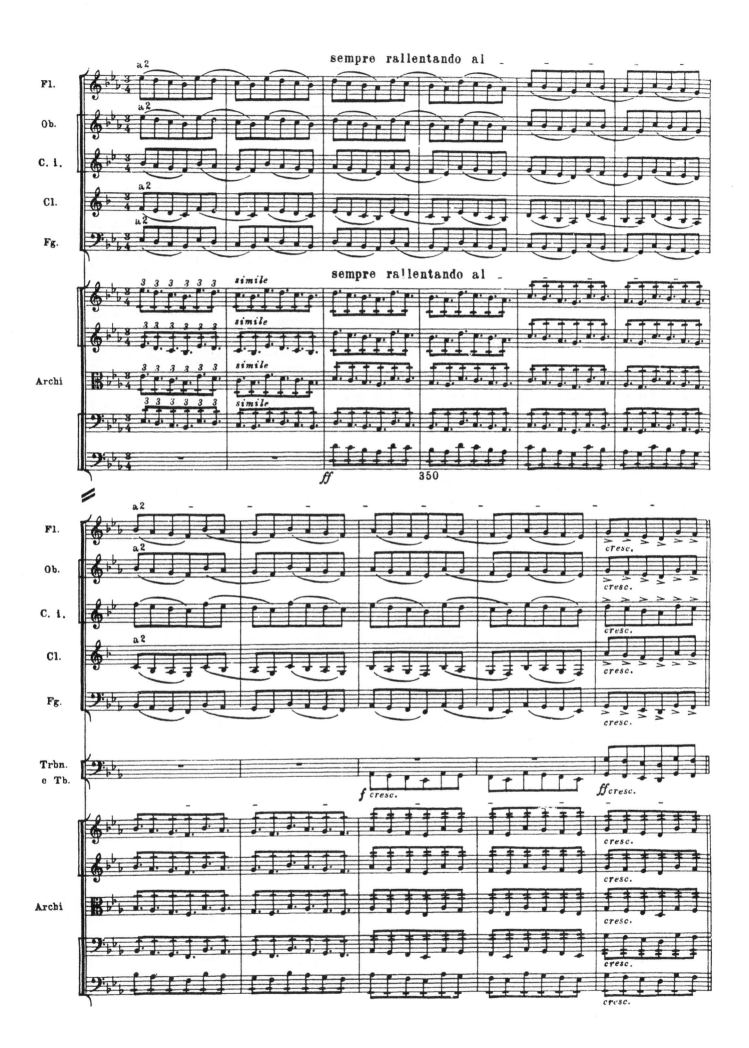

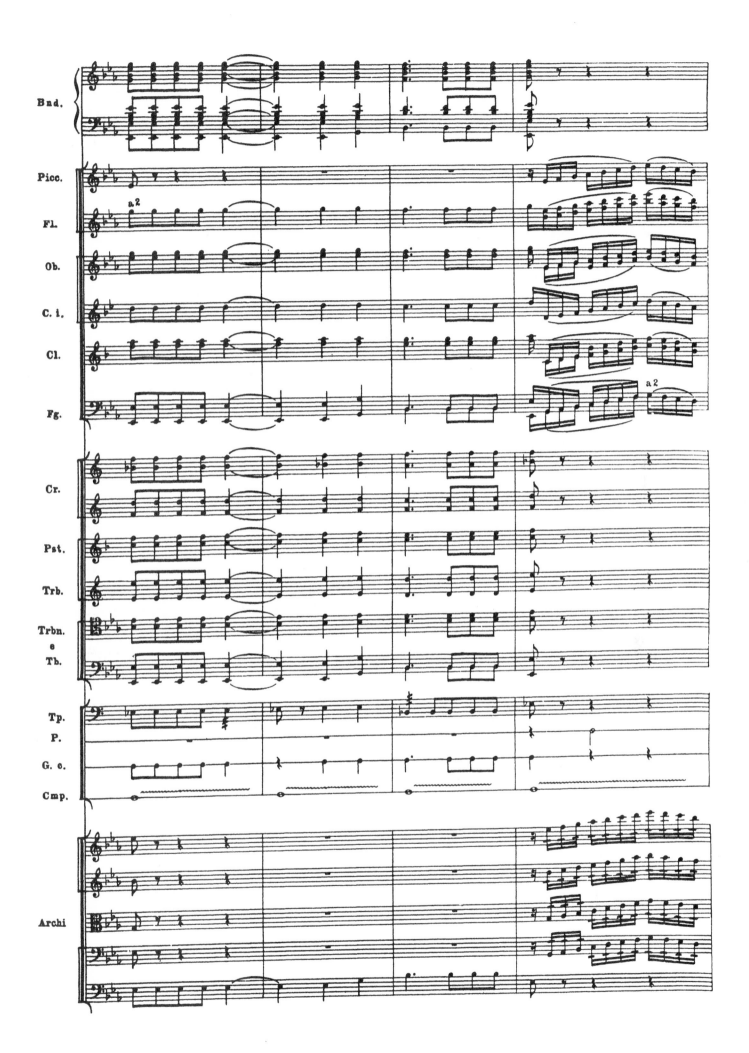

400

1) T.421 V.-I в автографе:
m. 421, V. I in the MS:

420

END OF EDITION